The Monster

Written by
Julie Hernandez , BA
NY State Retired CASAC,
Certified Life Coach

Briley & Baxter Publications | Plymouth, Massachusetts

ISBN: 978-1-954819-02-3

Book Design: Stacy O'Halloran

Dedicated to my family and all other families
affected by the disease of addiction.

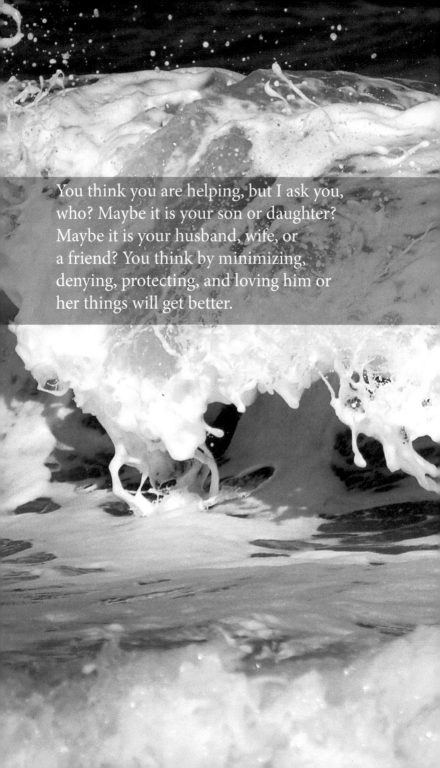

You think you are helping, but I ask you, who? Maybe it is your son or daughter? Maybe it is your husband, wife, or a friend? You think by minimizing, denying, protecting, and loving him or her things will get better.

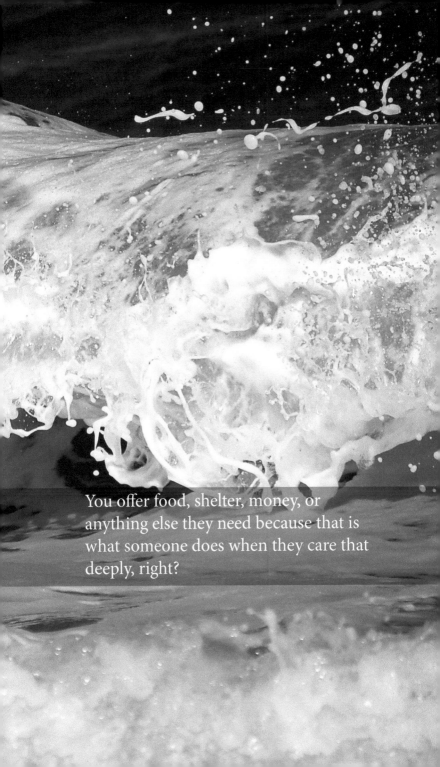

You offer food, shelter, money, or anything else they need because that is what someone does when they care that deeply, right?

But "it" grows stronger. You worry, you get angry, you beg, you plead, you throw guilt their way, and you even try a little tough love. Then, things get worse. You get sick, you think about them morning, noon, and night. You neglect and ignore other important people and things in your life. To the detriment of everything else, you are now obsessed with how to help.

Some of you go to counselors looking for answers—not for yourself but for how to better help your loved ones. You share your nightmare stories of what your loved ones do, how horribly they treat you, and how embarrassed you have been by them. You cannot believe they speak to you that way in private and in public. You just do not understand how they can cause so much pain to the people who love them so much.

You cannot fathom why they cannot see they have a problem and why they cannot just stop. You want to know what you did to cause their issues.

You tell the counselor about all the things you have done to help that are not working. You feel exhausted, frustrated, and powerless. You just do not know what else to do. You want to know why things just keep getting worse, why they hit you, verbally abuse you, hide things, steal, and lie to your face.

The counselor makes suggestions:

"Detach with love. Make a contract and stick to it. Stop keeping the secret. Stop protecting the addict from negative consequences. Go to Al-Anon. Find your spirituality, pray for guidance. Be around others who have been through the same adversities as you. They can help guide you with strength, hope, and the wisdom of their experiences.

You hear the counselor but just cannot follow through:

"What if I get her upset or angry and she drinks or drugs more? If I kick her out and something bad happens it will be my fault. What if she gets cold or hungry or hurt or worse yet—what if she dies?"

So, the counselor makes more suggestions...

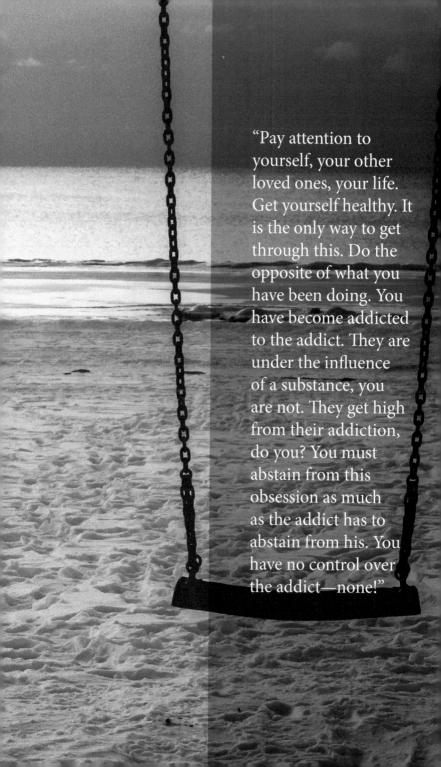

"Pay attention to yourself, your other loved ones, your life. Get yourself healthy. It is the only way to get through this. Do the opposite of what you have been doing. You have become addicted to the addict. They are under the influence of a substance, you are not. They get high from their addiction, do you? You must abstain from this obsession as much as the addict has to abstain from his. You have no control over the addict—none!"

When you continue looking the other way or accepting the unacceptable, you are, in fact, helping a monster. This monster lives inside of each and every addict. This monster is the disease of addiction.

So, if you really want to help, stop feeding the monster.

Stop loving and caring for him. Stop, because every time you think you are helping your loved one, you are, in fact, helping the monster grow stronger as your loved one grows weaker.

The monster disguises itself as
your loved one. It will say all the
right things to make you want
to keep helping, to make you
feel guilty, to manipulate you.

In time, the monster takes over
more and more. He tells your
loved one what to say and do.

- Ask for money. Tell them you need it for food, gas, or to feed your baby.
- Tell your parents you were out all night because you had to take your friend to the emergency room, and it was crowded.
- Tell them it is their fault you are like this. Blame anyone or anything that gets in your way.
- Threaten them any way you can. Tell them they will never see you again if you do not help.
- Tell them you are cold, sick, hungry, or in danger so they will take you back in.
- Cry, so they will feel bad for you.
- Tell them you love them. Tell them you're sorry and promise never to use again. This will buy you some time.
- When your mother asks you how you could have stolen her grandmother's wedding ring, act indignant and say, "how could you blame me for something like that?" Then storm out.
- Appeal to the weakest among them; they will keep helping even when the others "get it."

The monster's voice is continuous in their head. The monster's sole purpose is to get the alcohol or drug ingested into their body—only then does the monster rest. The monster quiets down for a while, until it is time for another feeding.

Your loved ones' bodies, minds, and souls are getting weaker, but, if you listen hard enough you can hear their inner cries for help...

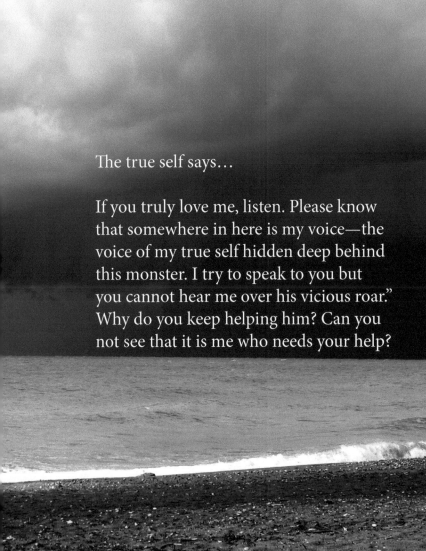

The true self says…

If you truly love me, listen. Please know
that somewhere in here is my voice—the
voice of my true self hidden deep behind
this monster. I try to speak to you but
you cannot hear me over his vicious roar."
Why do you keep helping him? Can you
not see that it is me who needs your help?

I cannot do this alone. I certainly cannot do this if you keep helping the monster ravish my body and mind. I am growing weaker every day. I will come back to you, but not this way, your way. I do love you, but I need you to hear my voice, to get yourself and me the right kind of help. I need to grow stronger because if I do not I may die.

If I won't get help right now, then wait for me. It may take me some time. I may have to go down a long hard path before I get better. When I am ready, I know that the only way I can do this is to admit that I need help from others who have travelled the same road before me.

I need help from God and yes, from you, to starve out this monster. So, if you can hear my voice, love me. I am still in here. Push me to go into treatment. Do an intervention. If I still won't stop, disconnect from me until I do. Make life hard for the monster, not easier. Appeal to me. No matter how loud the monster's voice is, I can still hear the loving whisper of yours.

Please have the answers on hand when I am ready to come to you for them. I need you to get yourself strong, because I am going to count on that strength when I need it. Make decisions as a family together. The monster will try to divide you. Do not allow it!

Please know that this is not about you.
It is not about what you did or did not
do or how you treated me in the past.
It is not about how much you love
me or what you think you did wrong.
The monster will use any weakness on
your part to kill me. Do not be fooled;
he is a cunning animal. With the right
kind of help, I can get better.

I have a higher power that is just waiting to take over where you leave off. Give Him a chance. God is the one who knows how to pull me through. I can faintly hear His voice too.

Most of you know that if I do lose this battle with the monster, if he wounds me, or causes me to wound someone else, it never was and never will be your fault. It was always the monster.

I never wished to cause you pain, worry, or grief. Please know that I did not choose this, it chose me. It is my lesson to learn from the universe. I will learn it as fast as I can and come back to you. In the meantime, please love and take care of yourself. I love you.